Transylvanian Deserts —My Mom's Recipes

Transylvanian Deserts —My Mom's Recipes

Nicoleta Popoviciu

Writers Club Press
San Jose New York Lincoln Shanghai

Transylvanian Deserts—My Mom's Recipes

Writers Club Press
an imprint of iUniverse, Inc.

For information address:
iUniverse, Inc.
5220 S. 16th St., Suite 200
Lincoln, NE 68512
www.iuniverse.com

ISBN: 0-595-21451-7

Printed in the United States of America

To my Mom

Contents

Thank you Cip and Simon !

Introduction

This book is a small collection of desert recipes gathered by my mother over the years. Its main goal is to ensure the preservation of these sweet treasures I grew up with in a Transylvanian city.

Scribbled in old school notebooks these recipes are some of our family's favourites. The collection was refined over the years through exchanges between my mother and her friends.

The notebooks are brought out of the cupboard for the Sunday deserts or sweet surprises for the kids. However, their magic is truly revealed on holidays, when trays and trays of cookies and cakes are readied for the visitors.

While sharing these recipes with you I hope to open a small window into the life of the people from this part of the world better known for its vampire stories than anything else. Nevertheless, it is fair to say that the Transylvanians have a sweet tooth too!

Transylvania

Friends and new acquaintances alike always enjoy my stories of Transylvania so I think you will too. A beautiful and rich land half ringed by the dramatic Carpathians, Transylvania has a long and tumultuous history. It was the last piece of the kingdom of the Daci to be conquered by the Roman Empire in the 105-106 AD campaign. This land was protected by the dense Carpathian forests and led the Romans to call it Trans-Sylvana (over the forest). The Roman settlers mixed with the local population and created a new people, the Romanians.

At the crossroads between Europe and Asia, Romania and Transylvania had to fend off many pillaging armies passing through. At the same time it benefited from the confluence of the eastern and western cultures.

The southern part of Romania adopted the Balkan, Greek, Turkish and Middle Eastern influences, the eastern part adopted the Russian ones, and Transylvania with its extended exposure to the Western European culture inherited its traits. All these influences are reflected in the local cuisine.

So what about Dracula and the Vampires? While the tall, dramatic mountains and the dark forests could easily support legends of the kind, Transylvania's vampire population is not higher that it is in other parts of the world. We owe our popularity to fictional literature…or so we like everyone to think.

Our family lives in and around the informal capital of Transylvania, the city of Cluj. Its roots can be traced back to the Roman city of Napoca. Cuddled between hills covered in orchards and close to the mountains, Cluj is a beautiful city with old buildings and quiet parks resting on the banks of river Somes. If you ever visit Romania, you have to stop in Cluj, the heart of Transylvania.

Deserts

The traditional Romanian deserts are generally based on yeast-raised dough complemented with fruits and preserves. A few of these deserts, typical for a farming society, are presented in the Cozonac chapter of this book. People still make them for holidays as tradition requires or, in the countryside, bake them on a regular basis along with the daily bread in ovens made of mud bricks.

Preserves are a very popular filling for Romanian deserts. Throughout the year each household makes delicious preserves out of various seasonal fruits. Diverse and flavour rich, the preserves allow one to add variety to a batch of cookies.

The more sophisticated deserts involving creams and chocolate were imported along the years and are extremely popular. The most common origins of some of these deserts are French, Hungarian and German. The recipes took a life of their own in the hands of creative moms so the above-mentioned notebooks contain many variations on the same theme. Each variation bares a name that concatenates the name of the desert and the name of the person it was acquired from. For example, the walnut cake recipe ends up with few variations such as: Walnut cake – Maria, Walnut cake – Nicoleta. For this book I selected the recipe I like the best out of each set.

In a Transylvanian household, the women cook the meals for the family. On the weekend, they make a large batch of desert meant to cover the Sunday lunch, where the entire family gathers, as well as the rest of the coming week. Some of these deserts do get better in time so nobody minds having them with coffee or milk few days after they were made. A good desert always lightens my day, so I hope this family treasure will bring you and your family the same joy.

Pofta buna! Bon appetite!

Chapter I

~ Coffee Cakes ~

Ecler

Chocolate and Vanilla Éclairs

Ingredients:

Dough:

½ litter Water
½ tsp. Salt
110 gr. (4 oz.) Butter
1 tsp. Sugar
220 gr. (8 oz.) Flour
5 Eggs

Filling:

Chocolate or vanilla pudding

Decorating:

Melted Chocolate

Utensils:

Cookie sheet

Preparation: *20 mins*

Cooking: *25-30 mins*

- *Mix the water, salt, butter and sugar*
- *Bring the mixture to a boil*
- *Add the flour by spoonfuls and stir to keep the mixture smooth*
- *Remove from the heat and let the mixture cool*
- *Add the egg yolks one by one to the flour mixture*
- *Whisk the egg whites and fold into the dough mixture*
- *Drop by tablespoons on cookie sheet, or use a pastry bag to give the desired shape*
- *Bake at 400 for 10 minutes, increase the heat to 425, and bake for an additional 15-20 minutes*
- *Let them cool before cutting, fill them with the pudding, and Spread a thin layer of melted chocolate on top*
- *For a more dramatic look you can pile the éclairs on your platter and then pour the melted chocolate on top*

An all time crowd pleaser, éclairs are a popular desert in many parts of the world. We make them small and round as opposed to the cylindrical shaped ones that are popular in the US. The éclairs will melt in your mouth so watch out for you might have a hard time getting away from them. The pudding filling can be replaced with whipping cream for more variety.

Prajitura Brinza

Ricotta Cheese Cake

Ingredients:

Dough:

1 ½ Cup Flour
200 gr. (7 oz.) Margarine
1 tsp. Baking Powder
1 Tbs. Cocoa
1 Cup Sugar
2 Egg Yolks
3 Tbs. Sour Cream

Filling:

800 gr. (28 oz.) Ricotta Cheese
3 Egg Yolks
2 Tbs. Semolina Flour
100 gr. (3.5 oz.) Sugar

Topping:

5 Egg Whites
5 Tbs. Powdered Sugar

Utensils:

12x9 Baking pan

Preparation: *30 mins*

Cooking: *1 hour*

- *Cream the margarine with the sugar and the cocoa*
- *Add the egg yolks, the sour cream and the baking powder*
- *Add the flour by spoonfuls*
- *Roll the dough out into a rectangle of the size of your baking pan*
- *Put the cake into the well greased and floured baking pan*
- *For the filling cream the eggs with the sugar, then add the rest of the ingredients*
- *Spread the filling on top of the cake*
- *Bake at 350 for 30 minutes*
- *For the topping, whisk the egg whites and add the sugar*
- *Take the cake out, and spread the topping on*
- *Put the cake back in the oven and bake for another 30 minutes*
- *Let the cake cool before cutting and serving*

Perfect for the cheese-lovers, this desert is a tasty alternative to a cheesecake. Like a cheesecake, it goes very well with fresh berries.

Prajitura Fructe

Fruit Topped Cake

Ingredients:

Dough:

4 Eggs
300 gr. (10.5 oz.) Sugar
4 Tbs. Boiling Water
100 ml. Oil
300 gr. (10.5 oz.) Flour
1 tsp. Baking Powder

Topping:

Fruits like pitted cherries, prunes, sliced apricots, peaches

Decorating:

Powdered Sugar

Utensils:

12x9 Baking pan

Preparation: 30 mins

Cooking: 35-40 mins

- Separate the eggs
- Whisk the egg whites
- Add the egg yolks
- Slowly fold into the egg mixture the rest of the dough ingredients
- Pour the dough into the well greased and floured baking pan
- Arrange the fruit on top of the cake
- Bake at 350 for 30-40 minutes until a cake tester comes out clean
- Let the cake cool before decorating with powdered sugar and slicing it

This easy to make desert can please everyone; just use their preferred choice of fruit for topping. Not too sweet, it is good for breakfast, to put in the lunchbox, or for an afternoon snack. This was mom's way out whenever we the kids pestered her for a desert.

Prajitura Cu Nuca

Walnut Cake

Ingredients:

Dough:

4 Egg Whites
140 gr. (5 oz.) Sugar
1 tsp. Baking Powder
100 gr. (3.5 oz.) Cake Flour
140 gr. (5 oz.) Butter
140 gr. (5 oz.) Chopped Walnuts

Topping1:

4 Egg yolks
150 gr. (5.25 oz.) Sugar

Topping2:

70 gr. (2.5 oz.) Butter
70 gr. (2.5 oz.) Sugar
70 gr. (2.5 oz.) Chopped Walnuts
3 Tbs. Cocoa Powder

Decorating:

50 gr. (1.75 oz.) Chopped Walnuts or Almonds

Utensils:

12x9 Baking pan

Preparation: 30 mins

Cooking: 35 mins

- For the dough, whisk the egg whites, then add the rest of the ingredients
- Pour the dough into the well greased and floured pan
- Cream the egg yolks with the sugar, and set aside
- Bake at 350 for 15-20 minutes; at this point the cake will not be fully cooked
- Take the cake out, and using a spatula spread the egg yolks mixture evenly on the cake
- Put the cake back in the oven and bake for an additional 10-15 minutes until the egg yolk mixture from the top hardens and a cake tester comes out clean
- For the second topping cream the butter with the sugar and the cocoa, and then add the walnuts
- Let the cake cool, and then using a spatula spread the second topping evenly on the cake
- Decorate with chopped walnuts or sliced almonds
- When ready to serve cut in small cubes and arrange on a platter

My mom's favourite, this desert is always part of our holiday menu. Extremely pretty, this cake will catch your eye and impress your taste buds.

Prajitura Cu Nuca

Roasted Walnut Cake

Ingredients:

Dough:

8 Egg Whites
6 Egg yolks
3 Tbs. Flour
140 gr. (5 oz.) Chopped Walnuts
140 gr. (5 oz.) Sugar
1 tsp. Vanilla extract
1 tsp. Baking powder

Topping:

50 gr. (1.75 oz.) Roasted chopped Walnuts
140 gr. (5 oz.) Sugar
2 Egg Yolks
200 gr. (7 oz.) Butter
2 Tbs. Finely Ground Coffee
¼ Cup Water

Decorating:

Melted Chocolate

Utensils:

Baking pan

Preparation: 30-40 mins

Cooking: 30 mins

- For the dough, whisk the egg whites, then add one by one the egg yolks
- Add the sugar, flour, and then the walnuts
- Add the vanilla and the baking powder
- Pour the dough into the well greased and floured pan
- Bake at 350 for 30 minutes until a cake tester comes out clean
- For the topping, cream the egg yolks with the sugar and the butter
- In a small saucepan bring the water to a boil, add the coffee, return to a boil, and set aside to cool
- Add 3-4 Tbs. of the prepared coffee to the topping mixture, and at the end add the walnuts
- Let the cake cool, and then using a spatula spread the topping evenly on the cake
- Spread a thin layer of melted chocolate on top of the cake
- Refrigerate until ready to serve

The perfect combination of coffee, walnuts and chocolate make this cake rise to any occasion. Serve it to your guests and they will not leave your house without asking for the recipe.

Prajitura Cu Stafide

Raisins Cake

Ingredients:

Dough:

7 Eggs
10 Tbs. Sugar
Zest and Juice from 1 lemon
1 Tbs. Baking Powder
100 gr. (3.5 oz.) Finely Chopped Walnuts
6 Tbs. Cake Flour
3 Tbs. Water

Topping:

100 gr. (3.5 oz.) Raisins
100 gr. (3.5 oz.) Rum
3 Eggs
6 Tbs. Sugar
200 gr. (7 oz.) Butter
200 gr. (7 oz.) Powdered Sugar

Decorating:

Grated Chocolate

Utensils:

Baking pan
Bain Marie

Preparation: 40 mins

Cooking: 30-35 minutes

- For the dough, separate the eggs
- Cream the sugar with the egg yolks
- Add the lemon zest and lemon juice
- Add the baking powder and the walnuts
- Whisk the egg whites with the water
- Add to the egg whites the flour, and mix everything together
- Pour the dough into the well greased and floured pan
- Bake at 350 for 30 minutes until a cake tester comes out clean
- Take the cake out and let it cool
- For the topping, soak the raisins in rum for at least 2 hours
- Using a Bain Marie whisk the eggs with the 6 Tbs. sugar
- Let the egg mixture cool
- Cream the butter with the sugar
- Combine the egg mixture with the butter one
- Drain the raisins, and add the raisins to the filling
- Spoon the filling over the cake, and decorate with grated chocolate

The delicate and light texture of the cake, with its lemon and walnut flavour is perfectly complemented by the chewy rum soaked raisins in the topping.

Chapter II

~ Cookies ~

Banuti

Meringue Sandwich Cookies

Ingredients:

Dough:

250-300 gr. (10.5 oz.) Flour
250 gr. (8.75 oz.) Butter
3 Egg yolks
1 tsp. Vanilla
2 tsp. Sour cream

Meringue:

250 gr. (8.75 oz.) Powdered sugar
3 Egg whites
Juice of 1 lemon

Filling:

Favorite fruit preserve
(Ours is apricot preserve)

Utensils:

Small Round Cookie cutter
Cookie sheets

Preparation: 35 mins

Cooking: 30 mins/batch

- Cream the butter
- Add the rest of the dough ingredients and mix well
- Roll the dough on wax paper into a 1/8 inch thick sheet
- Cut out the cookies using your cutter
- For the meringue whisk the egg whites until very stiff, then whisk in the sugar and the lemon juice
- Put the cut cookies on the cookie sheet and spoon the meringue on top of each cookie
- Bake at 300 for 30 minutes and then let them cool for 10 minutes
- Spread the preserve over bottom of 1 cookie, and press second cookie, bottom side down onto preserve

Perfect for the winter holidays, these cookies, because of their meringue top, look almost like snowballs. Sprinkled with powdered sugar, for a snowy effect, they are an elegant yet easy to make desert.

The versatility of this cookie does not stop here. For the calorie conscious folks, the meringue top can be eliminated, leaving a sugarless cookie filled with ones favourite preserve.

The halves of the cookies can be served individually. They are a delicious treat, very good for a big crowd, and hard to stay away from.

Biscuiti

Easy to make Tea Cookies

Ingredients:

Dough:

1 kg. Flour
3 Eggs
500 gr. (17.5 oz.) Margarine
3-4 Tbs. Sour Cream
1 ½ Cup of Sugar
1 tsp. Baking Powder
1 tsp. Vanilla
1 tsp. Grated Lemon

Filling:

Fruit preserve

Utensils:

Cookie cutter
Cookie sheets

Preparation: *30 mins*

Cooking: *15 mins/batch*

- *Cream the margarine with the sugar*
- *Add the eggs one by one and mix well*
- *Add the remaining ingredients*
- *Roll the dough on wax paper into a 1/8 inch thick sheet*
- *Cut out the cookies using your cutter*
- *Put the cut cookies on the greased cookie sheet*
- *Bake at 350 for 10-15minutes*
- *Spread the preserve over bottom of 1 cookie, and press second cookie, bottom side down onto preserve.*

Easy to make, these cookies are a favorite everyday accompaniment for your cup of tea, milk, or coffee. One batch would last your family a couple of days.

Biscuiti Nuca

Walnut and Coffee Sandwich Cookies

Ingredients:

Dough:

8 Egg whites
300 gr. (10.5 oz.) Powdered Sugar
300 gr. (10.5 oz.) finely chopped Walnuts

Filling:

8 Egg yolks
200 gr. (7 oz.) Sugar
100 ml. Brewed Coffee
1 Tbs. Flour
200 gr. (7 oz.) Butter

Decorating:

Chopped Walnuts

Utensils:

Bain Marie
Cookie sheets

Preparation: 40 mins

Cooking: 10-15 mins/batch

- Whisk the egg whites, and using a spatula, slowly fold in the sugar and the walnuts
- Spoon the dough on a greased cookie sheet. Use a spoon or a teaspoon in accordance to the desired size
- Bake at 325 for 10-15 minutes
- Cream the egg yolks with 100 gr. (3.5 oz.) sugar using a Bain Marie
- Mix the coffee with the flour and add to the egg yolks
- Cream the butter with the remaining 100 gr. (3.5 oz.) sugar
- Let the egg mixture cool a bit and then slowly add the creamed butter by the spoonful
- Fill the cookies
- Roll each filled cookie in the chopped walnuts

A light and crisp desert, these cookies are melting in your mouth. Depending on the chosen size, they can be presented on a platter or individually served a la mode.

Cornulete Nuca

Walnuts Crescents

Ingredients:

Dough:

200 gr. (7 oz.) Flour
150-200 gr. (7 oz.) Finely chopped walnuts
200 gr. (7 oz.) Butter
150 gr. (5.25 oz.) Powdered sugar
1 tsp. Baking powder
1 tsp. Vanilla

Decorating:

Powdered sugar

Utensils:

Pizza cutter
Cookie sheets

Preparation: 40 mins

Cooking: 15-20 mins/batch

- Cream the butter with the sugar
- Add the rest of the dough ingredients and mix well
- Let the dough rise for ½- 1 hour
- Roll the dough on wax paper into 1/8 inch thick, 10-inch diameter circles
- Cut each circle into 6 wedges, and roll up each wedge.
- Put the crescents on the greased cookie sheet. Curve ends to form crescent.
- Bake at 350 for 15-20 minutes
- Let the crescents cool.
- Decorate with powdered sugar

These cookies are a treat for the walnut lover. They have a crumbly texture, a rich walnut flavour, and a delicate hint of vanilla. The sugar powdered crescents look very elegant and ready for any occasion.

Cornulete Umplute

Filled Crescents

Ingredients:

Dough:

1 kg. (2.1 lb.) Flour
400 gr. (14 oz.) Lard or margarine
2 Egg yolks
1 Grated lemon
2 Tbs. of Yeast
½ cup of Milk
3 Tbs. of Sugar
½ tsp Salt

Filling:

Dried fruit, Turkish delight
Plum marmalade

Utensils:

Pizza cutter
Cookie sheets

Preparation: 40 mins

Cooking: 15-20 mins/batch

- Warm the milk and add to it the sugar and the yeast
- Let the milk mixture sit for a couple of minutes
- Combine all the other ingredients, add the milk mixture, and knead the dough well
- Let the dough rise for 1-2 hours
- Roll the dough into 1/8 inch thick, 10-inch diameter circles
- Cut circle into 6 wedges, put a piece of dried fruit or Turkish delight on each wedge, and roll them up.
- Put the crescents on the greased cookie sheet. Curve ends to form crescent.
- Bake at 350 for 15-20 minutes
- Let the crescents cool, and decorate with powdered sugar

A very traditional Transylvanian desert, these crescents are amongst my favorites. With the many filling options available, they can satisfy a wide taste range. Have a couple while they are still warm!

Islere

Chocolate Sandwich Cookies

Ingredients:

Dough:

500 gr. (17.5 oz.) Flour
200 gr. (7 oz.) Butter
1 Egg
3 Tbs. Sour Cream
1 tsp. Baking powder
1 tsp. Lemon juice
1 tsp. Vanilla

Filling:

200 gr. (7 oz.) Butter
200 gr. (7 oz.) Powdered sugar
3 Tbs. Cocoa powder

Decorating:

Melted chocolate

Utensils:

Round cookie cutter
Cookie sheets

Preparation: *40 mins*

Cooking: *15-17 mins/batch*

- *Cream the butter*
- *Add the rest of the dough ingredients and mix well*
- *If dough feels dry add another spoon of butter or sour cream*
- *Roll the dough onto wax paper into a 1/8-1/4 inch thick sheet*
- *Cut out the cookies using your cutter*
- *Put the cut cookies on the greased cookie sheet*
- *Bake at 350 for 15 minutes, and let the cookies cool*
- *Cream the butter with the sugar and the cocoa powder*
- *Fill the cookies*
- *Cover the top of the cookie sandwich with melted chocolate*
- *Better if made one or two days ahead, so the cookies soften a bit*

These elegant cookies are perfect for any holiday, or special occasion. They can be decorated with white, dark chocolate, or a combination of both for a marbled effect. The dough is sugarless; the calorie conscious can use them to sandwich a thin layer of fruit preserve.

Chapter III

~ Pound Cakes ~

Check cu Anason

Glazed Anise Pound Cake

Ingredients:

Dough:

400 gr. (14 oz.) Sugar
50 gr. (1.75 oz.) Cocoa
250 gr. (8.75 oz.) Butter
50 ml. Milk
1 tsp. Anise

---

3 Eggs
1 Cup Flour
1 Tbs. Baking Powder

Utensils:

Loaf Baking pan

Preparation: *40 mins*

Cooking: *30-40 mins*

- *Combine the sugar, cocoa, butter, milk and anise*
- *Put on low heat and mix often until everything melts*
- *Put aside 6 Tbs. of the above mixture, it will be used as the glaze*
- *Separate the eggs*
- *Whisk the egg whites in a separate bowl*
- *Add the eggs yolks, the flour and the baking powder to the melted mixture*
- *Fold in the egg whites*
- *Bake at 350 for 30-40 minutes until a cake tester comes out clean*
- *Let the cake cool a bit and glaze*

Check cu Mere

Cinnamon Apple Pound Cake

Ingredients:

Dough:

1 kg. (2.2 lb.) Apples
200 gr. (7 oz.) Sugar
2 tsp. Cinnamon

---

150 gr. (5.25 oz.) Margarine
250 gr. (8.75 oz.) Sugar
2 Eggs
500 gr. (17.5 oz) Flour
2 Tbs. Cocoa
1 tsp. Baking Powder
½ cup Nuts and Raisins

Utensils:

Loaf Baking Pans

Preparation: 40 mins

Cooking: 30-35 mins

- Peel, core and grate the apples
- Mix well with the sugar and the cinnamon
- Cream the margarine with the sugar, add the eggs, and mix well
- Add the rest of the dough ingredients and mix well
- Pour into the greased and floured baking pans
- Heat the oven at 425
- Put the cake in and immediately reduce the heat at 350.
- Bake at 350 for 30-40 minutes until a cake tester comes out clean
- Let the cake cool before cutting and serving

Use a couple smaller loaf pans or muffin pans and share this cake with your neighbours. Can be decorated with powdered sugar.

Check

Basic Pound Cake

Ingredients:

Dough:

10 Tbs. Flour
10 Tbs. Sugar
10 Tbs. Oil
10 Tbs. Milk
3 Eggs
1 tsp. Baking powder
2 tsp. Cocoa powder

Utensils:

Loaf Baking pan

Preparation: 20 mins

Cooking: 30-40 mins

- Cream the eggs with the sugar
- Add the rest of the dough ingredients and mix well
- Grease and flour the baking pan
- Pour 2/3 of the dough into your pan
- Mix the cocoa into the remaining dough, and pour it into the baking pan in swirls for a marbled effect
- Bake at 350 for 30-40 minutes until a cake tester comes out clean
- Let the cake cool before cutting and serving

Moist and delicious, this is a very easy to make pound cake. Can be served plain, or with your favorite ice cream along with fresh strawberries and chocolate syrup.

Check Pudrat

Powdered Pound Cake

Ingredients:

Dough:

250 gr. (8.75 oz.) Margarine
6 Tbs. Sugar
6 Eggs
1 Tbs. Baking Powder
6 Tbs. Flour
3 Tbs. Cocoa

Decorating:

Powdered Sugar

Utensils:
Loaf Baking Pan

Preparation: 20 mins

Cooking: 30-40 mins

- Cream the margarine with the sugar
- Separate the eggs
- Add the egg yolks one by one to the creamed margarine
- Whisk the egg whites in a separate bowl
- Combine all the dough ingredients and at the end fold in the whisked egg whites
- Pour into a greased and floured baking pan
- Bake at 350 for 30-40 minutes until a cake tester comes out clean
- Cut the cake while still warm and cover each slice with powdered sugar

This is a more elegant version of the pound cake. After slicing, using shaped cookie cutters (like stars, hearts, etc.) one can make this cake appropriate for special occasions like Christmas or Valentine's Day. Roll each piece in powdered sugar and arrange on a platter.

Check cu Stafide

Lemon-Raisins Pound Cake

Ingredients:

Dough:

4 Eggs
1 Cup of Sugar
1 Cup of Flour
1 tsp. Baking Powder
Zest from 1 lemon
½ Cup Raisins
2 Tbs. Cocoa

Utensils:

Loaf Baking pan

Preparation: *20 mins*

Cooking: *30-40 mins*

- *Separate the eggs*
- *Whisk the egg whites*
- *In a separate bowl cream the eggs yolks with the sugar*
- *Add the rest of the dough ingredients except the cocoa to the yolk mixture and mix well*
- *Fold in the egg whites*
- *Pour 2/3 of the dough into a greased and floured baking pan*
- *Mix the cocoa into the remaining dough, and pour it into the baking pan in swirls for a marbled effect*
- *Bake at 350 for 30-40 minutes until a cake tester comes out clean*
- *Let the cake cool before cutting and serving*

Prajitura Nuca Cocos

Coconut and Chocolate Cubes

Ingredients:

Dough:

125 gr. (4.4 oz.) Margarine
2 Eggs
8 Tbs. Milk
300 gr. (10.5 oz.) Sugar
1 tsp. Baking Powder
4 Tbs. Honey
Flour –as needed (see preparation)

Syrup:

1 Cup Milk
200 gr. (7 oz.) Sugar
200 gr. (7 oz.) Butter
3 Tbs. Powdered cocoa

Decorating:

Coconut flakes

Utensils:

12x9 Baking pan

Preparation: *20 mins*

Cooking: *30 mins*

- *Cream the margarine with the sugar*
- *Add the eggs and mix well*
- *Add the rest of the dough ingredients*
- *Add flour till the mixture thickens a little bit*
- *Pour the dough into a greased and floured baking pan*
- *Bake at 350 for 25-30 minutes until a cake tester comes out clean*
- *Let the cake cool and cut into 2 inch cubes*
- *Mix the syrup ingredients and bring to a boil, and keep it on low heat until it thickens*
- *Roll the cake pieces in syrup and then in the coconut flakes*

Kids will love this desert; they usually enjoy helping rolling the cubes in syrup and coconut as well.

Chapter IV

~ Very Traditional Deserts ~

For as long as I can remember, the walnut and poppy seed rolls were my favorite deserts. They still are the first things that come to mind when thinking of the holidays.

Days before Christmas my mom's small kitchen seems to be huffing and puffing because of all the cooking. Pots are simmering on the stove, and the oven bakes batch after batch of cookies. Away from the cold winter weather, the steamy kitchen filled with joyful conversation is the best place to be.

My mom's skilful hands knead the dough, while the rest of us crack open the walnuts and finely chop them. Spread over tables and cabinets, baking sheets full of glazed and filled dough wait their turn to the oven. They come out carrying the plump and golden deserts steaming hot and rich in flavor. The irresistible aroma draws everyone to the busy kitchen. It always ends up being a great time for the entire family. Kids always get to try the first slices while the Cozonac is still warm.

Whether filled with walnuts, poppy seeds, raisins, or dried fruit, whether yeast risen or not, whether roll or cylindrical in shape, these deserts are representative for the Romanian cuisine. Less sophisticated but delicious the Cozonac is sure to give you the joy of a good desert and the hard to define feeling of… "being home".

Cozonac Dospit

Walnut and Poppy Seed Rolls

Ingredients:

Dough:

1 kg. (2.1 lb.) Flour
50 ml. Oil
100 gr. (3.5 oz.) Butter
5 Eggs
3 Tbs. Sugar
2 tsp. Yeast
½ Cup of warm milk
2 tsp. Lemon zest
½ tsp. Salt

Filling:

½ kg. (17.5 oz.) Finely chopped Walnuts
100 gr. (3.5 oz.) Sugar
Or
Prepared Poppy Seed filling

Utensils:

Loaf baking pans

Preparation: 50 mins

Cooking: 40 mins

- Combine the yeast with milk and sugar and let it sit for 5 minutes
- Separate the eggs, and mix the egg yolks with all the dough ingredients and with the yeast and milk
- Knit the dough for a couple of minutes, and let the dough rise for 2-3 hours
- For the filling, whisk the egg whites and mix with the walnuts and the sugar
- Separate the dough into 2, and roll each part out into a rectangle of ½ inch thickness, and of length equal to your loaf pans
- Spread half of the filling on each rectangle and roll
- Let the rolls sit in the pans for 10-15 minutes
- Brush the rolls with 1 whisked egg yolk
- Bake at 350 for 30-40 minutes

Cozonac Nedospit

Walnut and Poppy Seed Rolls

Ingredients:

Dough:

700 gr. (24.5 oz.) Flour
150 gr. (5.25 oz.) Margarine
5 Eggs
4 Tbs. Sugar
2 tsp. Yeast
½ Cup of warm milk
2 tsp. Lemon zest
½ tsp. Salt

Filling:

½ kg. (17.5 oz.) Finely chopped Walnuts
100 gr. (3.5 oz.) Sugar
Or
Prepared Poppy Seed filling

Utensils:

Loaf baking pans

Preparation: 50 mins

Cooking: 30-40 mins

- Combine the yeast with milk and sugar and let it sit for 5 minutes
- Separate the eggs, and mix the egg yolks with all the dough ingredients and with the yeast and milk
- Knit the dough for a couple of minutes
- For the filling, whisk the egg whites and mix with the walnuts and the sugar
- Separate the dough into 4-6 parts, and roll each part out into a rectangle of ½ inch thickness, and of length equal to your loaf pans
- Spread filling on each rectangle and roll
- Grease the pans, put the rolls in and let them rise for 2-3 hours
- Brush the rolls with 1-2 whisked egg yolk
- Bake at 350 for 30-40 minutes

Placinta

Filled Fried Dough

Ingredients:

Dough:

1 kg. (2.1 lb.) Flour
1 Egg
100 ml. Milk
2 Tbs. Yeast
3 Tbs. Sugar
½ Tbs. Salt
1 Cup Water

Filling:

Grated Mozzarella Cheese
Dried Pitted Prunes, Apricots

Utensils:

Deep Frying Pan

Preparation: 50 mins

Cooking: 40 mins

- Combine the yeast with milk and sugar and let it sit for 5 minutes
- Mix the dry ingredients with the yeast mixture
- Add water as needed until the dough is not sticking and is easy to work with
- Knit the dough for a couple of minutes, and let the dough rise for 2-3 hours
- Get a handful of dough and roll into a circle of ¼ inch thickness
- On half of the circle spread the filling, fold the other half over, and seal
- Heat the oil in the frying pan and fry for 5 minutes or until a bit brown on each side
- Repeat with the remaining dough and filling
- Eat them while still hot!

The filling can be eliminated; after rolling the dough one can use a round cookie cutter, fry the round pieces of dough and then roll them in powdered sugar.

Chapter V

~ Layered Cakes ~

Crèmes Frantuzesc

French Crèmes

Ingredients:

Dough:

300 gr. (10.5 oz.) Flour
4 Tbs. Sour Cream
1 tsp. Baking Powder
100 gr. (3.5 oz.) Butter

Filling:

300 gr. (10.5 oz.) Sugar
1 tsp. Vanilla
80 gr. (2.8 oz.) Flour
500 gr. (17.5 oz.) Milk
350 gr. (12.4 oz.) Butter
3 Tbs. Cocoa

Decorating:

Powdered Sugar

Utensils:

Small Cookie Sheets

Preparation: 30 mins

Cooking: 15-20 mins/layer

- Cream the butter, add the sour cream, and mix well
- Slowly add the dry ingredients of the dough
- Separate the dough into 3 parts
- Roll each part on top of wax paper, into a rectangle as large as your cookie sheet
- Bake at 350 for 15-20 minutes
- For the filling mix the flour and the sugar, and then slowly add the milk and the vanilla, mixing well so no lumps are formed
- Bring the filling mixture to a boil, reduce heat and mix well till it thickens
- Let the egg mixture cool a bit and then slowly add the creamed butter to it
- Separate the filling into 2 parts, in one of them mix the cocoa
- Spread the cocoa filling on one layer of the cake, put a second layer on top of it, spread the rest of the filling on it, and then top it with the last layer
- Decorate with powdered sugar
- Better if made 1 day ahead

Foi Cafea

Coffee Filled Layered Cake

Ingredients:

Dough:

300 gr. (10.5 oz.) Flour
150 gr. (5.25 oz.) Margarine
2 Tbs. Sugar
2 Tbs. Sour cream
1 tsp. Baking powder
1 Egg

Filling:

4 Eggs
150 gr. (5.25 oz.) Sugar
100 gr. (3.5 oz.) Water
2 Tbs. Finely Ground Coffee
1 tsp. Vanilla
1 Tbs. Flour
200 gr. (7 oz.) Butter

Decorating:

Melted chocolate

Utensils:

Small Cookie Sheets

Preparation: 40 mins

Cooking: 10-12 mins/layer

- Cream the margarine with the sugar and the sour cream
- Add the egg and the rest of the dough ingredients and mix well
- Split the dough into 4 parts
- Roll each part on top of wax paper, into a rectangle as large as your cookie sheet
- Bake at 350 for 10-12 minutes
- For the filling bring the water to a boil, add the coffee, bring to a boil, and set aside to cool
- Cream the eggs with the sugar, add the vanilla, and then add the cooled coffee mixture alternating with the flour
- Bring the filling mixture to a boil, reduce heat and mix well till it thickens like a pudding
- Let the egg mixture cool a bit and then slowly add the creamed butter to it
- Spread 1/3 of the filling on one cake layer, put a second cake layer on top of it, and repeat with the rest of the layers and filling
- Spread a thin layer of melted chocolate on top of the cake
- When ready to serve cut into small squares

Foi umplute cu nuca

Walnut Layered Cake

Ingredients:

Dough:

200 gr. (7 oz.) Flour
190 gr. (6.7 oz.) Butter
150 gr. (5.25 oz.) Powdered Sugar
7 Egg Yolks

Filling:

200 gr. (7 oz.) Finely chopped Walnuts
100 ml. Milk
150 gr. (5.25 oz.) Sugar

Decorating:

Melted Chocolate

Utensils:

Small Cookie Sheets

Preparation: 40 mins

Cooking: 10-12 mins/layer

- Cream the butter with the sugar
- Add the egg yolks one by one, then the flour, and mix well
- Split the dough into 3 parts
- Roll each part into a rectangle as large as your cookie sheet
- Bake at 350 for 10-12 minutes
- For the filling bring the milk to a boil, add to it the sugar and the walnuts, and mix well
- Let the filling mixture cool
- Spread 1/2 of the filling on one cake layer, put a second cake layer on top of it, and repeat with the rest of the layers and filling
- Decorate with melted chocolate
- When ready to serve cut in small cubes

Prajitura Foaie Sfarmata

Crumbled Layer Cake

Ingredients:

Dough:

600 gr. (21 oz.) Flour
250 gr. (8.75 oz.) Butter
100 gr. (3.5 oz.) Powdered sugar
1 Egg
1 tsp. Baking Powder
2 Tbs. Sour Cream

Filling:

250 gr. (8.75 oz.) Sugar
250 ml. Water
250 gr. (8.75 oz.) Chopped Walnuts
1 Tbs. Apricot Preserve
3 Tbs. Cocoa
1 Tbs. Rum

Decorating:

Powdered Sugar

Utensils:

Small Cookie Sheets

Preparation: 40 mins

Cooking: 10-15 mins/layer

- Cream the butter with the sugar
- Add the egg, the rest of the dough ingredients, and mix well
- If the dough feels dry add more sour cream
- Split the dough into 3 parts
- Roll each part on wax paper into a rectangle as large as your cookie sheet
- Bake at 350 for 10-15 minutes
- For the filling make a syrup from the sugar and the water
- Break into small pieces one of the layers, and mix with the syrup
- Add the rest of the filling ingredients
- Spread the filling on one cake layer, put the second cake layer on top of it
- Decorate with powdered sugar

Chapter VI

~ Cakes ~

Savarine

Savarines

Ingredients:

Dough:

6 Eggs
6 Tbs. Sugar
6 Tbs. Plain Breadcrumbs
1 Tbs. Flour
1 tsp. Baking Powder

Syrup:

2 Cup Water
¾ Cup Sugar
2 Tbs. Vanilla/Almond Extract

Decorating:

Whipped Cream

Utensils:

Large Muffin Pan

Preparation: 15 mins

Cooking: 20 mins

- Separate the eggs
- Cream the egg yolks with the sugar, add the breadcrumbs, the flour and the Baking powder
- Whisk the egg whites and slowly fold into the above mixture
- Pour the dough into the muffin pan
- Bake at 350 for 10 minutes, reduce the heat to 250 and bake for an additional 10 minutes
- Let the savarines cool a bit, then remove from the pan and put into a deeper dish
- For the syrup boil the water with the sugar and at the end add the vanilla extract
- The syrup can be prepared using one's favorite flavor
- Let the syrup cool then pour over the savarines and refrigerate
- When ready to serve put on individual plates and decorate with whipped cream
- The savarines can also be baked in small loaf pans or any shape pans; I like to use heart shaped ones for Valentine's Day

Most likely you have never tasted a softer and lighter desert.

Tort Betiv

Drunken Cake

Ingredients:

Dough:

200 gr. (7 oz.) Butter
200 gr. (7 oz.) Powdered Sugar
3 Tbs. Cocoa
1 Cup Chopped Nuts
1 Cup Sour Cherries
4 Tbs. Kirsch
2 Eggs

Decorating:

Whipped Cream
Chopped Nuts

Utensils:

Mold

Preparation: *20 mins*

Chilling: *2 hours*

- *Cream the butter with the sugar and the cocoa*
- *Add the eggs along with the kirsch and mix well*
- *Add the nuts and the cherries to the mixture*
- *Put the cake mixture in a mold, which is padded with wet cellophane to prevent the cake from sticking*
- *Put the cake in the refrigerator to chill for at least a couple of hours*
- *When ready to serve turn the cake upside down on the serving platter*
- *Decorate with freshly whipped cream and chopped nuts*

Tort de mere

Upside down Apple Cake

Ingredients:

Dough:

6 Eggs
10 Tbs. Sugar
1 tsp. Baking Powder
6 Tbs. Flour
Cinnamon
6-7 Apples
Couple of Walnut Pieces for each Apple

Decorating:

Whipped Cream

Utensils:
Round Cake Pan

Preparation: 40 mins

Cooking: 1hour

- Spread 4 Tbs. of sugar on the bottom of the baking pan
- Core and peel the apples
- Arrange the apples in the baking pan in one single layer
- Fill the apples with walnuts and sprinkle with cinnamon
- Bake at 350 for 30-40 minutes until the apples are soft
- Cream the egg yolks with the remaining sugar
- Add the flour and the baking powder
- Whisk the egg whites and slowly fold into the above mixture
- Pour the dough on top of the apples
- Bake at 350 for 10 minutes, reduce the heat to 250 and bake for an additional 10-15 minutes
- Let the cake cool
- Turn the cake upside down on a platter and decorate with whipped cream
- Refrigerate until ready to serve

You will love this cake for it is bringing out the best of baked apples. It is the midway between the apple pie and a fancy cake.

Tort de portocale

Orange Walnut Cake

Ingredients:

Dough 1:
6 Eggs
6 Tbs. Sugar
6 Tbs. Flour
1 tsp. Baking Powder

Dough 2:
6 Egg Whites
250 gr. (8.75 oz.) Sugar
150 gr. (5.25 oz.) Finely Chopped Walnuts
3 Tbs. Flour
1 Tbs. Cocoa

Filling:
6 Egg Yolks
200 gr. (7 oz.) Sugar
3 tbs. Flour
300 ml. Milk
Orange zest from 1 orange
300 gr. (10.5 oz.) Butter

Decorating:
Powdered Sugar
Whipped Cream

Utensils:
Round Baking Pan

Preparation: 40 mins

Cooking: 1hour

- For Dough 1: cream the egg yolks with the sugar
- Add the flour and the baking powder
- Whisk the egg whites and slowly fold into the dough mixture
- Bake at 350 for 20-25 minutes until a cake tester comes out clean
- For Dough 2: whisk the egg whites and slowly fold in the other ingredients
- Bake at 350 for 25-30 minutes until a cake tester comes out clean
- For the filling cream the egg yolks with the sugar, add the flour and the orange zest, and at the end add the milk
- Bring the mixture to a boil, reduce the heat and mix until the filling thickens like a pudding
- Let the mixture cool and mix with the creamed butter
- Spread the filling on top of the first cake, top with the second one, and decorate with powdered sugar or whipped cream
- Refrigerate until ready to serve

About the Author

Born in the Transylvanian city of Cluj Napoca, Nicoleta Popoviciu is a Duke University graduate student. She moved to the United States in 1995 and currently resides in North Carolina. She enjoys cooking, and traveling.

0-595-21451-7

Printed in the United States
39504LVS00005B/385-387

9 780595 214518